TEN LANDSCAPES

ROCKPORT

TEN LANDSCAPES

TOPHER DELANEY

EDITED BY JAMES GRAYSON TRULOVE

GLOUCESTER MASSACHUSETTS

ROCKPORT PUBLISHERS

First published in the United States of America by:
Rockport Publishers, Inc.
33 Commercial Street
Gloucester, Massachusetts 01930-5089
Telephone: (978) 282-9590
Facsimile: (978) 283-2742

ISBN 1-56496-648-8

10 9 8 7 6 5 4 3 2 1

Book design: Toki Design (San Francisco)
Cover image: Ian Reeves

Printed in China

James Grayson Trulove is a magazine and book publisher and
editor in the fields of landscape architecture, art, graphic
design, and architecture. He has published, written, edited
over 30 books including, most recently, *New Design: Berlin,
New Design: Amsterdam, Designing the New Museum, Dancing in
the Landscape: The Sculpture of Athena Tacha*, and *The New American
Swimming Pool*. Trulove is a recipient of the Loeb Fellowship
from Harvard University's Graduate School of Design. He
resides in Washington, D.C.

CONTENTS

Personal life, expression, understanding, and history advance obliquely and not straight toward ends or concepts. What one deliberately seeks, he does not find; and he who on the contrary has in his meditative life known how to tap its spontaneous source never lacks for ideas and values.

Indirect Language and the Voices of Silence, Maurice Merleau-Ponty

Being in the world is a physical phenomenon, perceived through the experience of situations in the physical world. In this context, personal connection to the land, to the environment in which one dwells is intrinsic. For Topher Delaney, this philosophical understanding of being in and of the world is explored through the process of creating gardens. Interested in bringing forth perceptions of the senses and of time, the gardens that she creates begin with a process of discerning personal narratives, memories, and sense of place. The gardens speak through the language of "coded information". This language is not rhetorical; it is poetic and phenomenological. The code is a means of embodying place, one that uses form, material, and detail to translate information between the artist and the client. Topher Delaney interprets through an empirical process, searching for the "Promised Land" within the various personal narratives she encounters. She expresses the narrative studies by relating the memories, the hopes and yearnings for place, to render personal meaning onto the land. Transcending the realm of discourse, where intellectualism governs language

Topher Delaney enters the world of phenomenology and spirituality, where language is a means of communicating one's experience of being. It is a place where she speaks through the gardens, creating a world in which time and place are intimate.

Topher Delaney cultivates the land with purpose, blurring the boundaries between art, design, and construction. She is conscious of subverting the Hegelian categorization of "Art". From an early age, Topher Delaney was exposed to the art and "Art" world through her family. Pollock, Kline, Duchamp, and Noguchi among others, were personal friends of the family. To Topher Delaney, art is a part of everyday life, as lived by the artists she knew. It is also how she lives, where work and life are inseparable. Work only becomes "Art" through critique and validation, when it is institutionalized by discourse. Topher Delaney approaches her body of work as installations, where art and site are intrinsic to each narrative. In this medium, the "Art" cannot be extracted from the body, the place, the site. She is an artist with a populist agenda. It is a political statement, which is inherent in her affinity for issues of land. This conception stems from her other childhood experience, on a ranch in Wyoming, worlds apart from the zeitgeist of the Art culture in New York.

The cultivation of the "natural" necessitates an understanding of environmental elements for the growth cycles, equilibrium, and regeneration of living materials. It is an agrarian view of land, where culture is bound to the land. Topher Delaney cultivates the land as installations that speak of time, place and narrative. Beyond mere applique of surfaces and textures, the gardens are concerned with perceptions of land, of boundaries, and of light and shadow. The spatial intentions of the gardens construct an understanding of these perceptions. The weaving and cultivation of spatial intentions comes from her interpretation of individual narratives, belonging to her clients, which she translates as "coded information" within the text of the land. For Paul Gupta, a client whose memories are rooted in India, Topher Delaney translates his narrative from dialogues, bringing forth memories of experience; early connections with the land. The study and translation of the narrative is one of "coded information", where forms, movement, material, and detail render specific experiences. The process of creation is not arbitrary but comes from a tectonic translation of experience

scend the boundaries of private and public, sacred and profane, personal narrative and collective history. As a landed immigrant herself, Topher Delaney reflects upon the historically diverse cultural relationships to land. The "Promised Land" is a spiritual place, the Eden of dreams. The search for the "Promised Land" is expressed through reconstructed vignettes, embodied with personal memory and dreams of a future place, the Garden.

The history of the Garden reveals the relationship between people and their environment as expressed from spiritual or philosophical beliefs. The political, cultural, and social perception of nature is the groundwork that form expressions of the garden, from the romantic tradition of the English Garden, the formal tradition of the French Garden, the reserved tradition of the Zen Garden, to the abstract tradition of the Modern Garden. These typologies are relevant in their translation of particular narratives. Topher Delaney works with these typologies and reinterprets their relevance within specific narratives. Thus, the interest here is not historicism in a stylistic manner but rather an engagement of philosophical conversation. As in the fountains

of the Goldfarb garden and the Che Garden reveal, the use of historical forms references philosophical ideas. The Mannerist leitmotif of the Goldfarb fountain contains water in stasis, reinforcing the thick outlines of form. The Che fountain is a vessel of a perfect circle, from which water actively flow over the boundary of form. Each fountain refers to a different relationship of containment, revealing different philosophical perceptions of nature. The revelation of the history of Gardens is referential and speaks of the visible and the invisible allusions woven into the text of the land.

As a builder, the connection with the construction process is a means of direction over the medium of installation. Sculpting the land, form making required to create spatial configuration demands connection and understanding of the material, the physical. This is a crucial aspect of her work. Topher Delaney creates gardens that engage the senses, the experience of touch, sound, smell, and sight. The thoughtful choice of materials is particular to the site and the narrative. Materiality is revealed through the process and the relationship she engages with the personal narratives. Thus, the materials are not used contextually but experientially. Traditional materials are juxtaposed with modern materials without contradiction and irony. The use of fiber optics with glass boulders, the use of neon and glass against a backdrop of bamboo, these are examples that reflect the palette and composition of materials. For Topher Delaney, the use of plant material, stone, concrete, wood, metal, glass, and lighting are all active elements responsive to the natural forces of climate, light, shadow, and wind.

The situation always prevail. In what the senses of sight, hearing, and touch convey, in the sensations of color, sound, roughness, hardness, things move us bodily, in the literal meaning of the word.

—*The Origin of the Work of Art*, Martin Heidegger

In this time of our culture, where experience is increasingly mediated through mere imagery, through the screens of the electronic information age, the environment of our daily experience yearns for groundedness. The place we dwell, the physical environment, the home, is not an abstraction. Here, the sense of time is registered through light and shadow, the changing seasons, and the sense of place is the connection to the land. This is a fundamental reality of being. Time and place are interwined, experienced simultaneously. Materials as things are part of the experience of being. The work of Topher Delaney embraces the material, physical world, in their connection to the land, to the body. The gardens do not have a beginning nor an end, they are situations she has created in the continuum of place/time. The gardens will need to be tended, through the seasons of growth cycles. The subtleties of weathering will render upon the materials. The gardens continue to change through time. Outside, time cannot be captured but be observed. As an artist, creator of these gardens, Topher Delaney releases ownership, to the things, the environment, the narratives, and allows for the gardens to continue weaving onto the text of the land. The work of art becomes part of the everyday, the cycles, the personal narratives, the history of place. The "Promised Land" is implicit in the everyday, not a far away place. It is here; it is now.

KOAN: A RIDDLE IN THE FORM OF A PARADOX USED IN ZEN

CHE GARDEN

This garden sanctuary creates a harmonious environment for the contemplation of the koan. What is the source of the water's emanation? What is the power? Where is the beginning? Where is the end?

The process of revelation is imbued in the physical form of the garden. Discrete objects offer the opportunity to meditate on the exterior form of containment dissolving in the abstraction of nature to reveal the internal process of reflection. The vessel both contains and expresses the source of the flow of chi, water, and light.

Water mysteriously emanates from the vessel, an allusion to the constant replenishment of our own vessel, the soul. The form of the vessel is a metaphor for the process of discovery for the source of the flow and the illumination, which is embedded in the detail of our daily lives. The garden is defined by the inspiration of the client's spiritual beliefs, directing the location and form of the objects: a bench for sitting, a bowl for offerings, a terrace of crushed granite for listening. The cycle of seasons are marked by the transformation of the maple leaves as they shed and grow. Within this space, the philosophy of Buddhism amplifies and guides the formal structure of this garden wherein a dialogue is in constant transition between the illusory, the spiritual, and the visible form of the environment.

ABOVE: *Detail of water flowing over the rim of the vessel, there is an absence of a visible device for the drainage of flowing water. Dappled patterns of poplar leaves lie on the decomposed granite.*
OPPOSITE PAGE: *Eight foot diameter cast black concrete bowl, pink neon illuminates the form. Bambusa oldhambii envelopes and diffuses the boundary of the garden.*

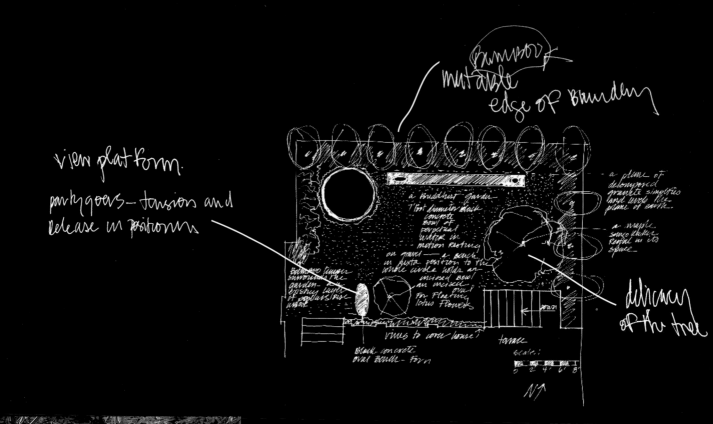

ABOVE: *A cherry tree is planted to form a canopy of blossoms over a cast black concrete oval "viewing" seat.*
OPPOSITE PAGE: *In the evening the form is revealed through the light. A twenty-foot linear black cast concrete bench with inset bowls for floating blossoms is located adjacent to the circular form of the fountain.*

STAMPER GARDEN

ABOVE: *Detail of "Rail of Perception"*

LEFT: *The vessel of water is submerged into a flat plane of grass punctuated by the thick trunk of birch.*

OPPOSITE PAGE ABOVE: *A cantilevered French limestone deck extends twenty feet over the existing grade.*

OPPOSITE PAGE BELOW: *Vertical rail pickets lay down in shadow across the French limestone terrace.*

ABOVE: *Spa with vertical glass wall. The surface of the water acts as a mutable mirror reflecting the picturesque.*
OPPOSITE PAGE: *Black academy granite forms a boundary installation by Edwin Hamilton. The graceful movement and texture of* Miscanthus gracillimus *contrasts the structural forms of stone.*

The focus of the garden's core is the "wild" land beyond the boundary of the internal geometric precision of limestone, grass, and water. This private garden, a mosaic of horizontal physical planes constitutes a viewing platform to the surrounding external public lands. the genesis of the spiritual philosophy which guides the formation of this garden is the obverse of the traditional walled sanctuary garden. The act of contemplation "of viewing" is expanded from the boundary of personal ownership, the edge of the suspended terrace, to a boundless panorama of "the wild." Here on this controlled green plinth of land one can meditate upon the uncontrolled complexity and beauty of the external. The intent of this internal garden is to recognize the extraordinary surrounding landmass through the literal elimination of the horizontal plane. Depending on one's angle of observation, the vertical pickets form a fan of visual perceptions from the open "invisible" to a solid boundary of definitions.

Within the frame of the ground plane a pool of water is set to form a horizontal surface which constantly ripples shifting the reflections of the sky. This body of water mirrors a streaming sequence of imagery which continually activates the core of the garden.

Adjacent to the entry garden, the threshold of transition between "the wild", the public woods, and the "ordered/controlled" private garden of contemplation is formed by the stacking of the wood removed through the original clearing of the land. The wall translates the process of removal/clearing and retrieval/reconstitution—the ultimate process of the garden—removal of the wild (nature untamed) and retrieval of nature tamed, the reformation of land into a syllabus of ornament, a style, the formal intervention of a garden.

OPPOSITE PAGE: *Detail of entrance wall.*
ABOVE: *Entrance sculptural stone wall by Edwin Hamilton.*

P A S S A G E

TO THE PRESENCE OF THAT WHICH IS ABSENT

GREENWICH GARDEN

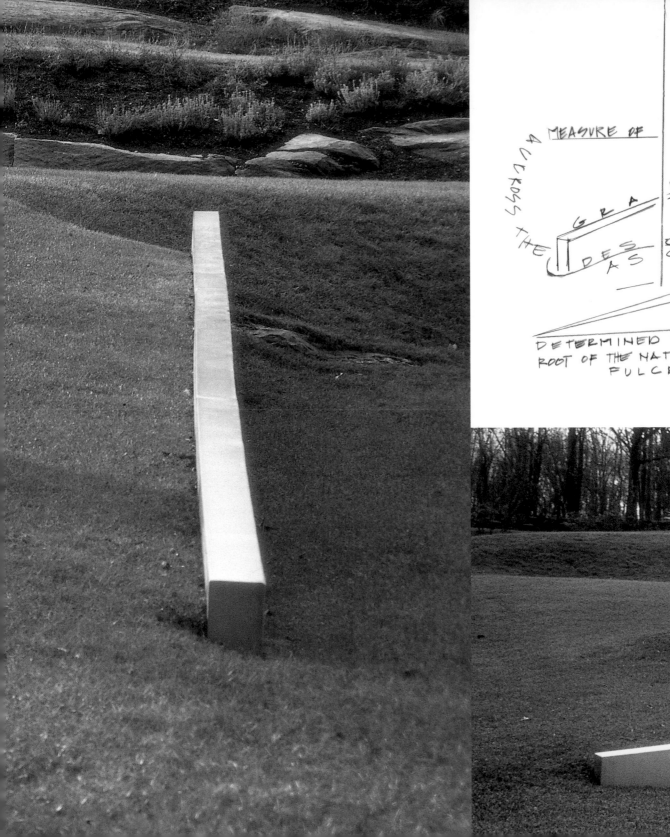

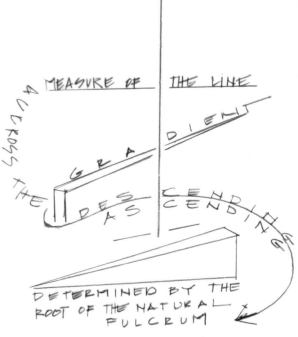

MEASURE OF THE LINE
ACROSS THE GRADIENT
DESCENDING
ASCENDING
DETERMINED BY THE
ROOT OF THE NATURAL
FULCRUM

This sequence of images depicts a cross section of land in three dimensions descending through the layered contours, a thin metallic strip of stainless steel demarks the "cross", further descent reveals the section—this manufactured geometry reinforces the placement of the vertical trunk of the central form of growth. This is the geometry of topography both in the vertical and the horizontal.

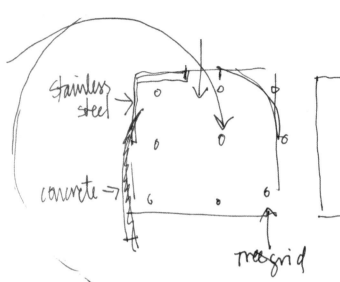

stainless
steel →

concrete →

treesgrid

house

A white plane of concrete scribes the topology of the land bisecting the triangular thrust of a stainless steel wedge. Calmagrostis "Karl Forster" grows through a slit of earth. The forms of a matrix of Fagus sylvatica "Atropunicea" *infuse an element of process within formal boundaries of the constructed landscape.*

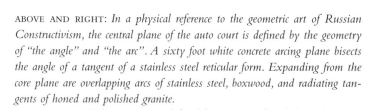

ABOVE AND RIGHT: *In a physical reference to the geometric art of Russian Constructivism, the central plane of the auto court is defined by the geometry of "the angle" and "the arc". A sixty foot white concrete arcing plane bisects the angle of a tangent of a stainless steel reticular form. Expanding from the core plane are overlapping arcs of stainless steel, boxwood, and radiating tangents of honed and polished granite.*

OPPOSITE PAGE: *The entrance is defined by a vector of asphalt and concrete which lodges into the form of the granite circle.*

Descending on the curve of the driveway, one passes through tangents of a boxwood circle to arrive within a central court defined by geometric forms. A pristine stainless steel triangular panel bisects a sixty-foot white concrete arcing plane. A seam of grass, Calmagrostis "Karl Forster" rises up between the intersection of these manufactured forms, a gesture, an act, which reflects the cycle of the seasons. Nine *Fagus sylvatica atropurpurea* are planted in a grid overlaying these discrete layers of metal and concrete modules to form a complex canopy of dappled branch patterns.

Tangentially located, the main entrance is paved in a compendium of geometric forms: honed granite and stainless steel. Longitudinal forms bisect the circle, a metaphor for the whole family infused with energy, the bisection of the line entering the sacred space.

In the rear garden, enveloped by the surrounding woods is a descending series of grass terraces punctuated by a triangle of stainless steel, arresting the flow of the arcs directly in front of the vertical form of the core/trunk of the largest tree. The gray furrowed bark of this tree, imperceptibly transforming with each season, contrasts with the immutable polished surface of the stainless triangle—a plinth of industry upholding the form of nature. Swaths of sedum, lavender, and chartreuse *Alchemilla mollis* roil the clipped surface and texture of the geometric ground planes of lawn. The device of the wall, the line of demarcation at the high point of the land, coupled with one's movement descending down around the "line", reveals the sculptural shift of the wall. This repetitive gesture in/on the land of the elevational modulations refers to the traditional device of the "HA HA", transformed in a contemporary interpretation of elevation—how we and from where we view a site—the shift of perception.

SO IN DARKNESS, SHALL WE

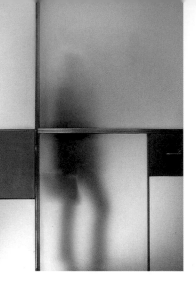

ABOVE LEFT: *Entrance—sandblasted glass and stainless steel.*

ABOVE RIGHT: *Entrance to garden—a vertical tapestry of trumpet vines grow on a stainless steel pole frame. The lighting mirrors the tube form of the poles.*

CENTER: *Central fountain is lit by fiberoptics, calla lilies grow from submerged planters. A set of formal white concrete stairs descend to the central courtyard.*

OPPOSITE PAGE RIGHT: *Central courtyard is located above a subterranean garage. Soil depth is four inches. Dichondra is planted in green strips between concrete paths.* Bambusa oldhamii *surrounds courtyard planted directly into the ground.*

choice
Dark — light
Compression — Release

Passing across the threshold, one is flanked by a redolent tapestry of green trumpet vines suspended on a grid of stainless steel. Located in the core of the entry garden is a white concrete square pool of water, a chalice of containment for miniature callas. Descending through a grove of olives one views a site-specific installation of two sandblasted glass walls backlit with white neon surrounding the central court. Defying the actual reality of the site, the central court is situated on the roof of a subterranean garage. This glass installation refers to the metaphor of our constant choice between darkness and light, the passive and the active both in our environment and our life. I believe we are always entering and descending into this forum. The entire installation is bounded by the natural growth of towering canes of *Bambusa oldhamii*.

As the cycle of daylight progresses to darkness, the glass boundaries radiate with a progressive intensity of light. Within darkness, the recessive is transmitted as an active vibration of light—"So in darkness, shall we find the light."

From the central plaza one presses up against the west concrete wall descending a narrow set of concrete steps to arrive in the internal garden of seclusion. Gravel forms a sonorous surface within the frame of the courtyard, white flowers of foxglove and iceberg roses fold over leaning across the expanses of flowerbeds. Planted in rusticate concrete planters balls of clipped green boxwood punctuate the horizontal plane of the white concrete walls.

OPPOSITE PAGE FIRST: *Each garden is sequestered by the protection of the wall. Hatch garden is located at the top of the photograph. Note spa and decomposed granite. The garden of reflection is located in the lower half of the photograph.*

OPPOSITE PAGE SECOND: *Boxwood spheres reinforce the linear structure of the wall. Inground lights are located to wash the wall with light.*

OPPOSITE PAGE THIRD: *East/west wall intersects south facing vine covered north wall. The text of the gravel covering the garden "floor" expresses subtle nuances of the colors, white and gray.*

OPPOSITE PAGE FOURTH: *The intersection—the corner forms the perception of the cloister. Parthenocissus tricuspidata grows across the chromatic surface of the ten-foot high white concrete wall.*

► 6

► 4

► 11

HATCH GARDEN

THERE ARE TWO WAYS OF SPREADING LIGHT: TO BE THE CANDLE OR THE MIRROR THAT REFLECTS IT. —EDITH WHARTON

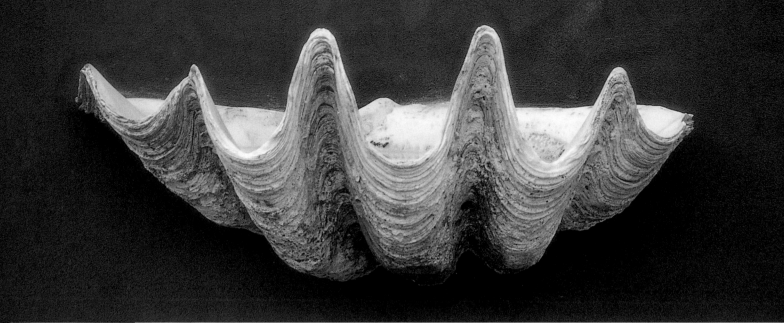

This white concrete wall defines the reality of two gardens considered and consummated at the same exact point in time. On the east side we developed "the garden of revelation" and on the west side we developed the Hatch garden. The physical form of the wall states by its very essence a proclamation of distinct individual interpretations: in contrast to clipped balls of boxwood on the east side, the west side is ornamented with mussel shells and mirrors set in a fleur de lys pattern. The glow of suspended candles emanates from the sienna and sulphur stained recessed niches.

Queen palms flutter their shadows on the text planes of the walls. The spa, the locus of abulations, is encrusted with shells patterned in a maritime jewel motif. Water flows over the extraordinary proportions of sculptural shells embedded in the violet walls. The foliage of giant birds of paradise fan the oval form of the spa. The wood walls, stained green, form the frame for white wisteria as it twists and whirls across the formal lines of the vertical plane. There is a sense of tranquility—the rustle of palm fronds, the sound of the water as it flows from a mysterious spring to an aqueous source of rejuvenation, the smell of citrus and roses, the flicker of candle light illuminating the sienna niches all contribute to form a cloistered sanctuary within the density of urban construction.

ABOVE: *The suspended shell is an allusion to the fonts found at the entrance to spiritual sanctuaries. The act of taking the water and blessing oneself is transferred to the act of literally washing the entire bod within "the spa." The shell is the well spring—the font of "purity"—pure water—thus in both a spiritual and sensual sense our equilibrium is restored through the experience of being in the garden.*
OPPOSITE INSET: *Oil sketch of the garden done as a study for the actual construction drawings.*

GARDEN OF

PACIFIC GARDEN

PREVIOUS PAGE LEFT: *Sculptural trumpets of light hang from the eucalyptus; a diaphanous stainless steel rail etches the edge of the deck of the upper public garden.*

PREVIOUS PAGE RIGHT UPPER: *Grass emanates from the top of the black stucco wall.*

previous page right middle and lower: The geometric shift of wood and concrete rectangles on axis descend down the curve of the steps.

BELOW: *Detail of "the discrete shift."*

OPPOSITE PAGE *The sequence of the geometric shift from public to private garden. On the north side of the steps an arced canted blue concrete wall lined with grasses and on the south a curving black stucco wall form the aperture of descent. No rails are required because the ground level has been elevated to step tread.*

This south facing urban garden, separated by a shift in elevation of fifteen feet, serves as a sanctuary for two distinct relationships: one of an immediate direct public nature and one of a sequestered intimate nature. On the upper elevation sweeping past six sets of French doors, a deck of ipe wood extends the flow of movement across the threshold of the internal to the external. Quite literally doors open to a room with a view. Suspended from the thick, gnarled trunk of the overhanging eucalyptus are fiberglass light cones which sway in the breeze creating animated circles of light on the surface of the deck. Planted to create privacy, surrounding this platform of wood, is a massing of *Bambusa oldhamii*, white Sombrieul roses, white Calla lilies, honey-suckle and ginger. A finely detailed stainless steel rail rims the curve of the deck, which is capped by a broad, flat band of stainless steel, on which to rest one's elbows, contemplating the sinuous shift from the macro view to the micro view of the garden.

Two curving sculptural walls of colored stucco frame the descent from the deck platform to the stone terrace adjacent to the pool. To the south of this serpentine staircase is a black wall which is bisected to create "a discrete shift"—an aperture through which to view the splaying arc of a blue concrete bench. A tufted line of grass emanates from the top of this wall with no apparent connection to the earth—a curious visual conundrum. Embedded in the text of descending steps is an intricate geometric text. Ipe wood laid on axis to both the black wall and the curve of the descent is enveloped by a black concrete square which is revealed in the descent. The corner of the concrete axis lifts to a form a triangle seat—pop-up geometry. Scented opulent trumpets of Brugmansia's white flowers hang over the canted blue concrete boundary wall of the descending steps.

OPPOSITE PAGE: *Canted and arcing concrete bench. Red lava dust and oil paving inset with variegated geraniums and sedum.*

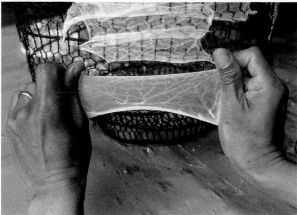

THIS PAGE: *How we form the surface—with pig gut and epoxy resin.*
OPPOSITE PAGE: *Suspended lanterns—illuminated by line voltage.*

Magenta bougainvillaea, lemons, bamboo, bananas, and gardenias envelop the lower garden. Anchoring the four-corners of the pool are concrete vessels planted with palms. The bottom of the pool is filled with loose blue pebbles, which diffuses the internal edges of the surfaces. The choice of palms reflects the visual repetition of an existing palm, which rises majestically up on the adjacent property. In the evening, the lower garden is defined by Chinese hanging lanterns, which emit orbs of soft yellow light creating a sense of an impending romantic celebration. Every night, a story is woven in the garden of Scheherazade.

OPPOSITE PAGE: *The cloistered garden enveloped by a rim of bamboo, bouganvillaea, solanum, and ivy. Necorema and jasmin in foreground flank the swimming pool. Suspended handmade Chinese lanterns cast a glow over the garden.*

GUPTA GARDEN

MEMOIR: A CONSIDERATION OF PERSONAL EVENTS WITH THE EVIDENCE OF A

POINT OF VIEW—A BIAS OF INTERPRETATION IN RELATION TO TIME AND SPACE.

This garden, created from a series of transcriptions, narratives and dialogues, sketches (on napkins, paperbags, concrete sacks,) and formal drawings reflects the invisible discursive process "of making." Paul and I talked about the possibilities of the imagined plot controlled by the restraint of the existing plot. We transcribed our forms—indices of our collaborative process over this text/land of fecund earth which is framed by six-foot fences, the boundary of serial development. Subdivisions laid down on the flats of "reclaimed" California marshlands—modulated by the "the master" developer to reflect the land, the grid, the pad.

Time and Text

The following questions were asked to evoke the client's spiritual, social, and physical history of personal terrain. All questions focused on the first seven years of his existence. It is my belief that these primal relationships to one's environment modulated by current events serve as a basis for significant interpersonal interpretations of a site. In a sense, we are all spiritual immigrants seeking the Promised Land. It is this specific search, to create an enclosure (garden) of a familiar paradise, which engages me in the act of investigating and creating the process of discovery, which determines a personal garden.

Where did you spend your first 7 years? Initially in an apartment (I am told), then at age three we moved to a single story house in middle class Delhi, India.

What are your young memories of your garden, what was the light like? I remember the back garden with banana trees in the side and my brother hitting the cricket ball in the trees, and the vegetable/melon vines and the earthworms in the rains. Sometimes we would look at the different kinds of ants, too.

What were the colors that you remember? Green, orange (gulmohar), yellow.

What plants do you remember? Banana, gourd/squash vines, gulmohar trees, lawn (we played in the back).

What did you do with your family in the garden? Cricket in the back (I would mostly watch), run around the back after homework.

What else do you remember? It was a semi-natural garden, I don't remember too much about any other relatives' gardens from back then. We had a small-boxy kind of garden.

What things did you not like about the garden? The earthworms. Sometimes they came inside when it rained.

PREVIOUS PAGE LEFT: *Detail of wall with pink geraniums selected to emphasize the coloration of the vertical surfaces.*
PREVIOUS PAGE RIGHT: *Detail of circular wall with desert palm gravel. A niche placed directly at apex of the circle reveals "nature" growing rampant behind the wall.*
ABOVE: *Detail of rastra foam wall finished with integrally colored acrylic stucco. Salvia leucantha is planted as a cameo appearance of beauty in form, color, and texture. The aperture in the circle leads to an elevated garden of lavender, black sand, and eclectic perennials.*
OPPOSITE PAGE: *Dark blue stucco wall projects through the wall calling into question the discrete separation of volumetric garden rooms. This form signals the movement from one elevation to another.*

The Release

"When you had finished plastering the colors on the walls, I had a dream—that wild animals were twisting in motion."

"The fire colors are vibrant expressions, especially the orange and red hues. Fire is an important part of my life. It is a dynamic element in the equation of life. Fire is mutable. You can feed it and watch it grow. It is interactive, a dynamic form of interchange."

Paul places front and center a brazier, which burns (in control/under control), creating mutable shafts of light on the orange surfaces of the circular enclosure.

The Frame

This is both a pictorial garden (the frame of the garden) and a sensual garden (the immersion in the garden), which is appreciated from the physical internal home space and the visual internal— the eye of the beholder.

"I am always assessing the modulations of this space, which transports me to the sacred space of a unique sanctuary." —Paul Gupta

LEFT: *The circular garden room is located directly in front of the main living area which frames the central court garden in a wrap of vibrant colors—a sari of walls surrounding the visage of the core.*
RIGHT: *Detail of pink and green walls, the colors of which were selected after visiting and Indian fabric store.*

GARDEN OF HISTORICISM

THE IRONIC RECONSTRUCTIONS OF HISTORICAL LEITMOTIFS

This garden reflects separate but interlocking partitas composed at two distinct junctures in time: the rear garden in 1994 and the entry garden in 1999. The topology of the garden was developed collaboratively with our clients to reference a series of historical vignettes, which chronicles distinct spiritual and cultural attitudes of the garden.

This "chance" collaboration in time and space between the client and the artist is required to establish the formal process of creating a distinct garden. By hand, by form, we render in explicit language the reflection (internal) and emulation (external) of the spiritual nature of the garden. This is a garden devoted to the precepts of reflection and revelation within the context of a temperate climate and the gridded formal abstraction of nature—the "suburbs."

In reverse passage through the garden from the internal to the external, one leaves the trapezoidal mediation room (fifty feet in length, twenty-feet wide contracting to one-foot in width) through apertures ascending from one-foot to five-foot openings. The shadow of this trapezoidal room tracks across the shadow plane of decomposed granite flanked by the "American Rose Garden", ebullient with splashes of red, orange, lavender, and white colors. Located directly in front of this floral abundance is the sculptural installation of a linear processional composition of stained wood blocks rotating in form from the cube to the triangle—an allusion to both natural and mathematical processes of nature. Flanking the other side of the shadow plane is a terrace of pink marbleized concrete defined by saffron plaster walls, the reverse of which reveals vibrant chartreuse surfaces enclosing the "orangerie".

OPPOSITE PAGE: *The metaphor of glass reflects the relationship between the manufactured glass surfaces of the architecture and the congealed forms of glass in the land. The metamorphic and refractive properties of glass were selected as an allusion to the historical geologic metamorphosis of the stones of Royanjii; however, we are now in California with a currency of new technologies where rocks are transformed into glass lit by fiberoptics.*
ABOVE: *A sandblasted glass panel forms a translucent entrance to the threshold of the garden.*

Two planar celadon stucco walls define the shift from the decomposed granite court of the shadow plane to a terrace of honed black granite, which extends through the ground plane of the house to the entry garden adjacent to the street. A sole olive tree forms a dappled canopy over this reflective black surface. The leaf color mimics the shade tones of the architecture's glass walls. Planted on either side of this black formal terrace are two balanced planes of lavender bisected by gravel paths, which lead respectively to an herb garden and a fountain of water flowing over a glass disc. Walking past this fountain through the callas to the side garden we use the wheel path constructed to provide both a walk and a surface for the wheelbarrow filled with garden clippings to be wheeled through to the entry garden and the street.

In the entry garden we meter our step to a deliberate slow pace, our body in motion following a narrow sinuous ribbon of black concrete, "The Scholar's Walk", which curves through a plane of green baby's tears. Again, we walk on the rectilinear plane of black granite, which extends from the core of the garden through the house to the entry path ending at the public sidewalk. Punctuating

the monochromatic text of baby's tears glass orbs glowing kryptonite green positioned as allusions to Japanese gardens of contemplation such as Royanji, where the viewer contemplates nature through the abstraction of natural forms. The viewer is extant-exterior to the garden observing the external. The entry threshold of stainless steel and sandblasted glass both defines and deflects the light and shadow of the exterior street—the threshold of intersection between the profane (the external) and the sacred (the internal).

RIGHT: *The principle of kū-tei is investigated through the selection of material and form within the entry garden. The granite entry slab/path is an allusion to the viewing platform—a linear intervention flanked by the monochromatic text of baby's tears and glass gravel. This garden is viewed both in passage and internally from the core of the home.*
FOLLOWING PAGE LEFT: *Black concrete "wheelbarrow" path flanked by callas.*
FOLLOWING PAGE RIGHT: *Reflections on the black concrete "Scholar's Walk" set within a plane of baby's tears.*

FAR LEFT: *"The orangerie." The mellifluous scent of Seville oranges from potted citrus trees.*
LEFT: *Chartreuse walls of the orangerie, pink concrete terrace, decomposed granite on "the shadow plane" or petanque court, the perception of which depends on whether you are mediating or playing ball.*
BELOW: *Lavender "Goodwin Creek" is bisected by plaster celadon walls, a fruitless olive "Majestic Beauty" overlays the black granite terrace.*
BELOW RIGHT: *A field of lavender flanks the rear of the house. The tonality of the plant's leaves mimic the vertical tones of the architectures, silver, glass and stucco.*

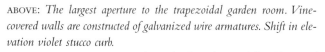

ABOVE: *The largest aperture to the trapezoidal garden room. Vine-covered walls are constructed of galvanized wire armatures. Shift in elevation violet stucco curb.*

RIGHT AND OPPOSITE PAGE: *The garden boundary is diffused by panel of vines punctuated by columns of Italian Cypresses. The elevated rose garden provides the plants with magnificent soil and drainage. The location facing south is optimum. The site specific installation of stained wood forms morph laterally from cube to triangle while maintaining a continuum of form in the frontal view. The "natural" appearance is a fiction—in nature there is no stasis of color or form.*

LEFT: *Looking north—"the trapezoidal garden room" lavender gravel from Barstow, California, walls diffused by the roil of bougainvillaea, trumpet vine and red blaze roses.*

RIGHT: *the shadow of the apertures transverse across the shadow plane of the composed granite. This room is created as a monumental* gnomon *which serves as both a resting place and a sculptural form which charts the shadow of the passage of light.*

OPPOSITE PAGE: *Looking south—the form of the room contracts from twenty-feet to the compression of one-foot. Views through the apertures.*

HARLEQUIN GARDEN

"Pay no attention to the man behind the curtain."
—The Wizard of Oz

This south-facing garden located to the right of the entrance to the house is directly adjacent to the elevated dining and family rooms. This installation focuses on the use of theatrical devices. Bisecting lines of a diamond pattern extend the visual length and width of the garden. Oversized, elevated steel planters hold wide brimmed date palms forming an immediate green canopy of intimacy. At the terminus of the garden the placement of mirror strips located at the apex of the steel plates dissolves the perception of the property's actual limits reflecting a garden that exists only in our imagination—calling into question the validity of the visual information we assume to be "real."

There is a balance of both traditional and contemporary gestures within the graphic form of this garden. These acts are revealed in the paving, a classic black and white harlequin pattern bounded by trapezoidal steel planters, the steel screens, the mirrors, and the cast-bronze Italianate fish, spitting water into a surreal clam shell filled with glass cullet. The flounce and drift of Sally Holmes roses, the thick forms date and sago palms and the confetti of perennial blooms envelop these discrete surfaces to create an intimate room for reverie.

ABOVE: *Sally Holmes roses cascade over an edge band of paving turned on its side. The balcony of the first floor overlooks the garden.*
OPPOSITE PAGE: *A cast iron Florentine fish spews water into a chalice of water. A mirror backing reflects the garden amplifying the diagonal pattern of the concrete tiles. Cold rolled steel panels form an impenetrable shoji screen. Mirror strips create the illusion of a garden which extends beyond.*

LEFT: *Trapezoidal cold rolled steel planters with grass, glass cullet, palms and candles.*
RIGHT: *Detail of a Sansevieria trifasciata with black and white concrete diamond edge bands.*
OPPOSITE PAGE: *Balconies extend into the garden flanked by raised steel planters of* Phoenix canariensis *to create a "room with a view."*

LEFT: *A marble panel is positioned as a site specific installation which alludes to a state of being—antithetical to the reference of this ceremonial marker of passage.*

OPPOSITE PAGE: *The topiary pot garden—a herd of rosemary, thyme, and bay are corralled by the front entrance tethered to the land by feet of clay.*

GOLDFARB GARDEN

"I am nature."
—Jackson Pollock

Often depicted through the medium of black and white photography, historical gardens lay bare their structures. We can easily trace form and content through this reduction of visual information. I chose to represent this garden in this format for the intrinsic reason of its creation, the "historical" re-creation of a garden. The intent was to extend and expound upon the existing form, a structure of distinctive brick architecture. The creation of a seamless connection between both the existing structure of the 1930s and the garden, created in 1978, was achieved through the verisimilitude of materials, which reflects the text and texture of the site structures.

Within this garden, seemingly traditional in its layout and use of materials, is the placement of a significant device of illusion, front and center, similar to the Harlequin Garden completed in 1998. The use of mirror illuminates and extends the perception of the exact dimensions of the garden. Both gardens are intimate in their scale and urban location. The historical framework of the garden is bisected directly in the center core by the mirror—an illusion and metaphor to imagination and to the question of perception—what is real and what is not real. The introduction of this device is the beginning of an investigation into aspects of coded information within the landscape of man.

LEFT: *Cast iron patinated rails rim the elevated tile terraces. Front and center is a mirror enveloped within the arch of the constructed brick rim walls.*

BELOW: *Cast concrete elevated koi pond. Brick clad metal arches support tile terraces with copper moulding panels.*
OPPOSITE PAGE: *Detail of mirror. Ficus tree hedge. Formal boxwood and herb garden. Handmade copper lights mimic the form of the arch.*
FOLLOWING PAGE LEFT: *Detail of Welsh tile on terrace.*
FOLLOWING PAGE RIGHT: *Handcast spiral staircase produced by Robinson Ironworks.*

BELOW: *New steel sash door with Welsh tile thresholds.*
OPPOSITE PAGE: *Musing on the reflections of the illusory.*

SELECTED GARDENS AND PROJECTS

CHE GARDEN, CALIFORNIA

Concrete contractor: Pasqual Castillo
(Richmond, CA)
Neon Contractor: Neon Neon
Materials: Vessel: formed black concrete;
Recessed light: pink neon; Ground
plane: decomposed roofing granite
Significant Plant Material: *Bambusa oldhamii;
Acer palmtum; Prunus serrulata*

STAMPER GARDEN, CALIFORNIA

Contractor: Owner
Stacked wood wall construction:
Anthony Rodrigues, Bruce Stamper
Black granite stone boundary sculpture:
Edwin Hamilton (represented by New
Leaf Gallery, 510 525-7621)
Gardener: Anthony Rodrigues, Bruce Stamper
Materials: Paving at pool deck: French limestone;
Paving at entry: decomposed granite;
Rails: powder-coated metal stanchions;
Pool: tempered glass panel
Significant plant material: *Quercus virginiana;
Miscanthus sinensis "Gracillimus";
Bambusa oldhamii*

GREENWHICH GARDEN, CONNECTICUT

Contractor: Owner
Materials: Walls: stainless steel; white concrete;
Paving: asphalt; Entrance paving:
flamed black granite; polished black
granite and stainless steel
Significant plant material: *Fagus sylvatica atropur-
purea;* Calmagrotis "Karl Forster";
Buxus sempervirens

KUHLING/WILCOX GARDEN, CALIFORNIA

Contractor: T. Delaney Inc./Jose Hildago
Metal/Glass Entrance Door: Doug Hellikson Design
and Manufacturing (Oakland, CA)
Lighting: fiberoptics; incandescent by Dan Dodt
(San Francisco, CA)
Gardners: Glenda Jones
Materials: glass cullet rocks; glass gravel; glass
bowl; Paving: honed black granite;
Black concrete paving; Felton Quarry
decomposed granite; Adequin lavendar
gravel; Stucco walls: acrylic integral
color; standard integral color; Painted
galvanized metal armatures of 4x4
hogwire mesh

Significant Plant Material: *Acer palmatum;* Italian
Cypress; *Cupressus semperirens;* Bougain-
villaea "Barbara Karst"; Lavandula
"Goodwin Creek"; *Bignonia Cherere;*
Climbing Rose "Blaze"

GARDEN OF REVELATION, CALIFORNIA

T. Delaney Inc. in partnership with Andrea Cochran
Contractor: Owner
Sandblasted Glass Wall: Steve Chambers
Lighting Mechanisms: Jeff Pilotte (San Francisco, CA)
Neon Installation: William Concannon (Benecia, CA)
Lighting Contractor: Dan Dodt (San Francisco, CA)
Materials: stainless steel armatures; white concrete
paving/walls; courtyard planters by
Luchiano (Carmel, CA, 813 624-9396)
Glass Wall: sandblasted tempered glass; mirrors;
black slate
Significant Plant Material: *Bignonia Cherere; Buxus
sempervirens; Olea europea* "Majestic
Beauty"; *Bambusa oldhamii*

HATCH GARDEN, CALIFORNIA

Contractor: T. Delaney, Inc.
Materials: Party wall: white concrete; pure pigment
stain; Stucco wall by spa: integral
color; Wall surrounding garden: 2x12
redwood stained with pure pigment;
Paving: decomposed granite
Surface Ornament: mussel shells; abalone shells;
conch shells
Significant Plant Material: Queen palms, *Syagrus
romanzoffianum*

PACIFIC GARDEN, CALIFORNIA

Contractor: T. Delaney, Inc./Jose Hildago
Concrete Planters: Mary Collins
Materials: Deck: ipe planks; Rails: stainless steel;
Stairs: ipe and integral color concrete;
Walls: integral color stucco; Bench:
integral color concrete; Light cones at
deck area: hand-made fiberglass sheath-
ing; Lights shades at garden area: hand-
made Chinese lanterns with gut and
epoxy
Significant Plant Material: *Bambusa oldhamii;
Brugmansia candida;* white standard;
Citrus; Bougainvillaea; *Ensete ventricosum;
Neomarica caerulea; Phoenix Canariensis*
in pots; on descending steps, Juncus
"Quartz Creek"; Sedum "Vera
Jameson"; *Carex testacea, Carex buchanii*

GUPTA GARDEN, CALIFORNIA

Contractor: Jose Hildago
Lighting: brazier with charcoal; brazier with wood
Materials: Walls: Rastra foam with footings; Surface:
La Habra acrylic stucco; Paving: desert
palm gravel
Significant Plant Material: *Michelia doltsopa; Salvia
leucantha;* gernaniums; *Lavender prineta*

HARLEQUIN GARDEN, CALIFORNIA

Contractor: T. Delaney, Inc/Jose Hildago
Materials: Paving: Buddy Rhodes Studio
(415 641-8070); Planters: tempered steel;
Walls: tempered steel, mirror; Glass:
residual cullet
Significant Plant Material: Sally Holmes roses;
Phoenix Canariensis; Dasylirion

GOLDFARB GARDEN, CALIFORNIA

T. Delaney, Inc.; consultant Pam Anela Messanger
Contractor: Richard Colton (Berkeley, CA)
Materials: Wall: used brick veneers; mirror; Paving:
brick; Rails: cast iron by Robinson Iron
Works; Spiral stairs: original cast iron by
Robinson Iron Works
Significant Plant Material: Ficus

PHOTOGRAPHY

Topher Delaney: pp. 7; 8; 10 (top); 15; 28–39; 42
(top); 50 (top); 64–71; 86; 107 (bottom)
Loretta Gargan: pp. 13–14; 16–17; 50 (bottom)
Jerry Harper: pp. 43 (top right); 46 (second left)
Michael Kenna: p. 9
Katherine MacDonald: p. 12
Lexi Milstein: p. 107 (top)
E.B. Min: p. 1
Ira Nowinski: pp. 10 (bottom); 18–27; 46–47; 49
(right); 51; 53; 62; 77–78; 88–104
John Peden: p. 42 (center)
Betsy Pinnover: p. 46
Ian Reeves: front cover, pp. 40–41; 42 (bottom); 43
(bottom right); 44–45; 48; 49 (left);
72–73; 80; 82; 87; 108
Kelli Yon: pp. 52; 54–61; 74–75; 77; 81; 83–85
Nina Zeigler (artist): p. 107 (center)

Movement
I think of direction, exterior passage through installations/
I am creating the art of circumstance.
First, I begin as a gardener—tending, planting, pruning
formal arrangements within the context of place and time.

I begin as a writer—I observe the datum noting the sequence
of events the conflicts and the resolutions.
I begin as an artist—I explore within the text of the land
through issues of memory, identity, absence, and presence.

Collaborative Installations—Partnerships with the intention
to scribe within the existing canvas symbolic interventions—
of form which transcends the static to evolve through the
revolution of cultural and seasonal cycles.

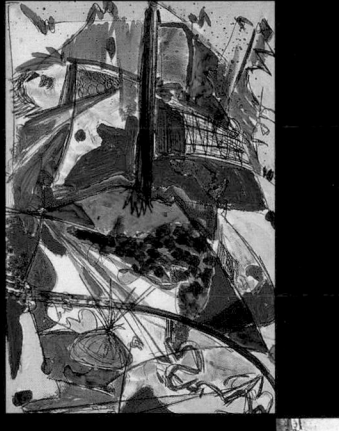

Station
Studio, 156 South Park in San Francisco. Exhibition space, library, computers, music,
layout tables, chalk drawings on the floor, watercolors, arrangements of materials, stirring
discussions, lists, dates, phones, directions, many people coming/going.